J O N A H
The Inside Story

written and illustrated by Heidi Petach

To my mother,
Billie Augsburger,
who taught me to love God,
my neighbor, and a good story.

Second Edition, 1995
Library of Congress Catalog Card Number 88-63567
© 1989, The Standard Publishing Company, Cincinnati, Ohio
A division of Standex International Corporation. Printed in U.S.A.

Long, long ago God talked to a man called Jonah.

"Jonah," He said, "I want you to go to the great city of Nineveh. Tell the people there that I am tired of seeing them be so mean."

"What!" cried Jonah, surprised. "I can't go there! The people of Nineveh are bullies. They have been doing bad things to my friends and neighbors for a long time."

Nineveh was the last place on earth Jonah wanted to go.

So instead of obeying God and going to the big city of Nineveh, Jonah left on a ship that was sailing in the opposite direction – all the way across the sea to Tarshish.

But God was watching Jonah. He sent a great wind to blow the sea into huge, rocking waves. Whoosh! The ship was tossed about like a tiny toy.

The sailors were afraid the boat would sink because of the heavy load it carried, so they threw the cargo overboard into the sea.

Everyone on the ship was frightened.
Everyone except Jonah. Where was he?
Fast asleep, snoring!

"Wake up!" shouted the ship's captain. "How can you sleep at a time like this? Call on your God to save us!"

But Jonah wouldn't. He was trying to run away from God.

Splash! Crash! The storm got worse. The people decided God was punishing someone on the ship. They drew straws to see who it was. The one who pulled the shortest straw would be the guilty one. Guess who pulled it?

"I'm the one," Jonah admitted. "God is angry with me for disobeying Him. Throw me overboard and the storm will go away."

But the sailors didn't throw Jonah overboard. Instead, they rowed hard to bring the ship back to land as the wind roared louder and the waves rolled higher.

Finally the sailors were so afraid that they gave up and threw Jonah overboard into the sea.

Was this the end of Jonah? No. God had a plan to save him.

Deep, deep down in the sea lived a huge, fish-like creature. God had made it especially to take care of Jonah.

Luckily the sea creature obeyed God better than Jonah did. With a big gulp, it swallowed Jonah whole so he wouldn't drown.

For three days and three nights
Jonah lived inside the huge animal
where it was like a dark, slippery cave.

But Jonah prayed while he was inside
the creature. He thanked God that he
was alive.

Then God spoke to the big sea
creature and told it to spit Jonah out
on a beach. It was glad to get rid of
Jonah. Jonah gave it a tummyache!

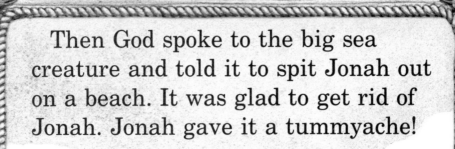

Finally Jonah obeyed God and went to the city of Nineveh and preached to the people. Jonah said, "In forty days God will flatten your city because you have been acting so mean!"

Then the people of Nineveh were sorry they had been so bad. Even the king himself believed in God and promised to be better.

This made God very happy. He was glad He didn't have to destroy the city and could save the people of Nineveh.

But Jonah wasn't happy at all. He had liked feeling better than the people of Nineveh. He didn't want God to forgive them.

Hoping God would change his mind and flatten Nineveh after all, Jonah sat outside the city and waited to see what would happen next.

Soon the sun was high overhead, heating Jonah till he felt like he was sizzling in a frying pan.

To cool off, poor Jonah built a tent-like shelter for shade. Meanwhile, God made a vine to grow up and shade Jonah even more. What a relief! Jonah felt a lot better then.

But the next day God sent a hungry worm to eat the vine.

This made Jonah angry and he cried out, "Lord, why did you let that poor plant die?"

Then God told Jonah, "You felt sorry for the plant, but you don't want me to feel sorry for the people of Nineveh. Shouldn't I forgive those who turn to me, no matter who they are?"

Finally Jonah understood what God had been trying to teach him. He went back home and wrote this story telling us how much God loves *everyone*.

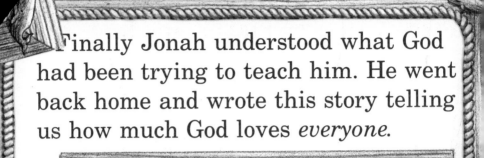